Introduction

Welcome to a world where pizza transcends its humble origins and becomes an unparalleled masterpiece. In "Pizza Perfection," embark on a culinary journey that will revolutionize your pizza-making skills and elevate your appreciation for this beloved dish. From amateurs seeking to impress their friends to seasoned cooks looking to refine their craft, this book is the key to unlocking a realm of pizza excellence.

"Pizza Perfection" unveils the secrets to achieving flawless pies in the comfort of your own kitchen. Immerse yourself in the artistry of dough, learning the delicate balance of ingredients, kneading techniques, and rising times that yield a crust that's crisp on the outside yet wonderfully tender within. With expert guidance, you'll conquer different dough styles, from Neapolitan and Sicilian to thin-crust and gluten-free options, ensuring that every bite delivers pure satisfaction.

But a truly exceptional pizza is more than just its base. In this book, you'll explore the symphony of flavors that can be created through carefully curated toppings, sauces, and cheeses. Discover the alchemy of combining fresh and seasonal ingredients, experimenting with unique flavor combinations, and perfecting the balance of textures to create a slice that transcends the ordinary.

"Pizza Perfection" is not just a collection of recipes—it's a comprehensive guide that covers every aspect of the pizza-making process. Delve into the art of stretching and shaping dough, explore different cooking methods including wood-fired ovens and home pizza stones, and learn the secrets of achieving the ideal sauce-to-cheese ratio. With detailed step-by-step instructions and helpful tips, this book ensures that each pizza you create will be a masterpiece in its own right.

Whether you're craving a classic Margherita, a bold and inventive gourmet creation, or a comforting slice of nostalgia, "Pizza Perfection" has you covered. With its diverse range of recipes, inspiring photographs, and insightful techniques, this book will empower you to unleash your creativity and transform your kitchen into a pizzeria of your dreams.

Prepare to embark on a culinary adventure, where you'll perfect your dough, elevate your toppings, and create pizzas that will leave your taste buds singing with delight. With "Pizza Perfection" as your guide, your home will become a haven for pizza lovers, and your creations will forever be remembered as slices of pure perfection.

Homemade Margherita Pizza

Ingredients:

1 ½ cups all-purpose flour
1 teaspoon active dry yeast
1 teaspoon sugar
1 teaspoon salt
¾ cup warm water
2 tablespoons olive oil
1 cup tomato sauce
2 cups shredded mozzarella cheese
Fresh basil leaves
Salt and pepper to taste

Instructions:

In a small bowl, combine the warm water, sugar, and yeast. Stir gently and let it sit for about 5 minutes until the mixture becomes frothy.

In a large mixing bowl, combine the flour and salt. Make a well in the center and pour in the yeast mixture and olive oil. Stir everything together until a rough dough forms.

Transfer the dough onto a lightly floured surface and knead for about 5-7 minutes until the dough becomes smooth and elastic. If the dough is too sticky, add a little more flour.

Place the dough in a greased bowl and cover it with a clean kitchen towel. Allow it to rise in a warm place for about 1 hour or until it doubles in size.

Preheat your oven to 475°F (245°C). If you have a pizza stone, place it in the oven while it preheats.

Punch down the risen dough and divide it into two equal portions. Roll out each portion into a thin circle or your desired pizza shape.

Transfer the rolled-out dough onto a baking sheet or a pizza peel if using a pizza stone.

Spread half of the tomato sauce over each pizza base, leaving a small border around the edges. Sprinkle half of the shredded mozzarella cheese evenly over each pizza.

Place the pizzas in the preheated oven and bake for about 12-15 minutes, or until the crust is golden brown and the cheese is melted and bubbly.

Remove the pizzas from the oven and let them cool for a minute. Sprinkle fresh basil leaves on top and season with salt and pepper to taste.

Slice the Margherita pizzas and serve them hot. Enjoy!

Note: Feel free to add extra toppings like sliced tomatoes or fresh garlic if desired. Also, adjust the baking time as per your oven's instructions and personal preference for the crust's crispness.

Turkey Alfredo Pizza

Turkey Alfredo Pizza is a delicious Italian-style pizza that combines turkey, spinach, and creamy Alfredo sauce for an unforgettable meal. This delicious pizza recipe is incredibly easy to prepare and can be whipped up in no time.

To begin preparing this delicious pizza, preheat the oven to 425 degrees Fahrenheit. Place a prebaked 12-inch thin pizza crust on a baking sheet and set aside. Next, rub the cut side of a garlic clove onto the crust and spread ½ cup of reduced-fat Alfredo sauce over it.

In a medium bowl, combine thawed and squeezed dry frozen chopped spinach with lemon juice. Spread the mixture evenly over the prepared crust and sprinkle 2 cups of shredded cooked turkey breast over the spinach. Drizzle the remaining ¼ cup of Alfredo sauce over the turkey and top with 3/4 cup of shredded Parmesan cheese.

Place in preheated oven and bake for 15-18 minutes, or until pizza crust is golden brown and cheese is melted. Cut into slices and serve hot. Enjoy!

With just a few simple ingredients, you can now make delicious Turkey Alfredo Pizza right in your own home! Not only is this recipe delicious, it's easy to make and full of delicious flavors that will tantalize your taste buds. Try making this delicious pizza today and see how much your family loves it!

Best Ever Taco Pizza

Ingredients:
For the pizza dough:
2 ½ cups all-purpose flour
1 teaspoon instant yeast
1 teaspoon sugar
1 teaspoon salt
1 cup warm water
2 tablespoons olive oil

For the taco topping:

1 pound ground beef or chicken
1 small onion, diced
2 cloves garlic, minced
1 packet taco seasoning
½ cup tomato sauce
1 cup shredded cheddar cheese
1 cup shredded lettuce
1 cup diced tomatoes
½ cup sliced black olives
½ cup sliced jalapeños (optional)
Sour cream and salsa for serving

Instructions:

In a small bowl, combine warm water, sugar, and instant yeast. Stir gently and let it sit for about 5 minutes until the mixture becomes frothy.
In a large mixing bowl, combine the flour and salt. Make a well in the center and pour in the yeast mixture and olive oil. Stir everything together until a dough forms.
Transfer the dough onto a lightly floured surface and knead for about 5-7 minutes until the dough becomes smooth and elastic. If the dough is too sticky, add a little more flour.
Place the dough in a greased bowl and cover it with a clean kitchen towel. Allow it to rise in a warm place for about 1 hour or until it doubles in size.
While the dough is rising, preheat your oven to 425°F (220°C). If you have a pizza stone, place it in the oven while it preheats.
In a skillet, cook the ground beef or chicken over medium heat until browned. Add diced onion and minced garlic and cook until the onion is softened.
Stir in the taco seasoning and tomato sauce, and simmer for a few minutes until the flavors meld together. Remove from heat and set aside.
Once the dough has risen, punch it down and roll it out on a lightly floured surface into your desired pizza shape.
Transfer the rolled-out dough onto a baking sheet or a pizza peel if using a pizza stone.
Spread the taco meat mixture evenly over the pizza dough, leaving a small border around the edges.
Sprinkle shredded cheddar cheese over the taco meat.
Place the pizza in the preheated oven and bake for about 15-20 minutes, or until the crust is golden brown and the cheese is melted and bubbly.
Remove the pizza from the oven and let it cool for a minute. Top with shredded lettuce, diced tomatoes, sliced black olives, and sliced jalapeños if desired.
Slice the taco pizza and serve it hot with sour cream and salsa on the side.

Enjoy the Best Ever Taco Pizza!

Spinach Artichoke Pizza

For the pizza dough:
2 ½ cups all-purpose flour
1 teaspoon instant yeast
1 teaspoon sugar
1 teaspoon salt
1 cup warm water
2 tablespoons olive oil

For the spinach artichoke topping:
1 cup frozen spinach, thawed and squeezed dry
1 cup canned artichoke hearts, drained and chopped
4 cloves garlic, minced
½ cup cream cheese, softened
½ cup mayonnaise
½ cup grated Parmesan cheese
1 cup shredded mozzarella cheese
Salt and pepper to taste

Instructions:

In a small bowl, combine warm water, sugar, and instant yeast. Stir gently and let it sit for about 5 minutes until the mixture becomes frothy.
In a large mixing bowl, combine the flour and salt. Make a well in the center and pour in the yeast mixture and olive oil. Stir everything together until a dough forms.
Transfer the dough onto a lightly floured surface and knead for about 5-7 minutes until the dough becomes smooth and elastic. If the dough is too sticky, add a little more flour.
Place the dough in a greased bowl and cover it with a clean kitchen towel. Allow it to rise in a warm place for about 1 hour or until it doubles in size.
While the dough is rising, preheat your oven to 425°F (220°C). If you have a pizza stone, place it in the oven while it preheats.
In a medium bowl, mix together the cream cheese, mayonnaise, minced garlic, grated Parmesan cheese, salt, and pepper until well combined.
Once the dough has risen, punch it down and roll it out on a lightly floured surface into your desired pizza shape.
Transfer the rolled-out dough onto a baking sheet or a pizza peel if using a pizza stone.
Spread the cream cheese mixture evenly over the pizza dough, leaving a small border around the edges.
Sprinkle the thawed and squeezed dry spinach over the cream cheese mixture.
Top with chopped artichoke hearts.
Sprinkle shredded mozzarella cheese over the top.
Place the pizza in the preheated oven and bake for about 15-20 minutes, or until the crust is golden brown and the cheese is melted and bubbly.
Remove the pizza from the oven and let it cool for a minute. Slice the Spinach Artichoke Pizza and serve it hot.
Enjoy your delicious Spinach Artichoke Pizza!

Tomato Baguette Pizza

Ingredients

8 ounces sliced fresh mushrooms.
2 medium onions, halved and sliced.
2 garlic cloves, minced.
3/4 cup thinly sliced fresh basil leaves, divided.
3 medium tomatoes, sliced.
1/2 teaspoon Italian seasoning.
2 teaspoons olive oil.
1 French bread baguette (10-1/2 ounces), halved lengthwise.

This delicious pizza recipe is a great way to use up fresh tomatoes and baguettes. To prepare the pizza, preheat your oven to 375°F. In a large skillet, sauté mushrooms, onions, and garlic in olive oil until tender-crisp. Add 1/2 cup of basil leaves and Italian seasoning; cook for one minute more. Spread tomato slices over the cut sides of the baguette halves and top with mushroom mixture. Sprinkle remaining 1/4 cup of basil leaves over each half. Bake for 15 minutes or until heated through. Serve warm and enjoy! With this delicious pizza recipe, you can bring delicious flavors into your kitchen without having to leave home! Enjoy!

Seafood Pizza

Seafood pizza is a delicious and unique dish that will tantalize your taste buds with its delicious combination of flavors. This delicious pizza recipe starts off with 12 uncooked medium fresh shrimp, which are kept in their shells for added flavor. The base of this delicious seafood pizza is 1 cup of pizza sauce, followed by 1 cup of shredded mozzarella cheese (4 oz) and 1/2 cup of shredded provolone cheese (2 oz). To give the pizza an extra boost of flavor, 8 anchovy fillets in oil and 1/2 lb bay scallops are added. Finally, the dish is topped with a sprinkle of 1/2 cup chopped fresh basil leaves and 1/2 teaspoon pepper to enhance the flavor even further.

This delicious pizza recipe is easy to follow and can be prepared in just a few steps. First preheat your oven to 375°F and prepare a baking sheet with parchment paper or foil. Place the shrimp on the sheet and bake for about 8-10 minutes until cooked through. Once the shrimp are done cooking, remove them from the oven and let cool before preparing the rest of the pizza. Spread the pizza sauce over a pre-made or pre-bought crust, then sprinkle with both cheeses followed by anchovies, scallops, basil leaves, pepper, and finally cooked shrimp. Bake this delicious seafood pizza at 375°F for 12-15 minutes until golden brown. Enjoy!

For delicious pizza recipes that are sure to please, try out this delicious seafood pizza. With its combination of delicious ingredients and easy preparation steps, you'll be able to enjoy a delicious meal in no time!

Bacon Chicken Pizza

Making delicious pizza recipes at home is easier than you think! This bacon chicken pizza is packed with delicious flavors and takes only minutes to prepare. To get started, gather the following ingredients: 60g of shortcut bacon, sliced; 200g of wholemeal Lebanese bread; 125g tomato passata; 150g button mushrooms, thinly sliced; 1/2 medium red capsicum, thinly sliced; 1/2 medium red onion, thinly sliced; 200g cooked skinless chicken breast, shredded; and 1 cup reduced-fat mozzarella cheese, shredded.

To begin preparation for your delicious pizza recipe, preheat your oven to 220°C (200°C fan). Place the Lebanese bread on a baking tray lined with baking paper. Spread the tomato passata evenly over the bread, followed by the mushrooms, red capsicum and onion. Then top with the bacon and chicken. Finally, scatter the cheese over the pizza and bake for 20 minutes or until golden brown.

Your delicious bacon chicken pizza is now ready to be enjoyed! Serve hot or cold, it's guaranteed to make an impression on your guests this summer! Enjoy!

Buffalo Chicken Pizza

Ingredients

1 tube (13.8 ounces) refrigerated pizza crust.
1 cup Buffalo wing sauce, divided.
1-1/2 cups shredded cheddar cheese.
1-1/2 cups part-skim shredded mozzarella cheese.
2 pounds boneless skinless chicken breasts, cubed.
1/2 teaspoon each garlic salt, pepper and chili powder.
2 tablespoons butter.

This delicious buffalo chicken pizza recipe is the perfect way to bring together the spicy and tangy flavors of Buffalo wing sauce with delicious cheese and tender chunks of chicken. Start by unrolling the refrigerated pizza crust onto a greased baking sheet. Brush half of the Buffalo wing sauce over crust before adding a layer of cheeses, followed by cubed chicken that has been seasoned with garlic salt, pepper and chili powder. Finally, brush remaining wing sauce over top before baking for 12-15 minutes in an oven preheated to 425°F. Enjoy this delicious buffalo chicken pizza as is or serve with ranch dressing for extra deliciousness! The result will be a delicious, cheesy and spicy meal everyone will love! So why not give it a try and enjoy delicious pizza recipes at home? You won't be disappointed!

This buffalo chicken pizza is easy to prepare and the delicious result will make you glad you tried it. All you need to do is start by unrolling the refrigerated pizza crust onto a greased baking sheet, brush half of the Buffalo wing sauce over crust before adding a layer of cheeses, followed by cubed chicken that has been seasoned with garlic salt, pepper and chili powder. Finally, brush remaining wing sauce over top before baking for 12-15 minutes in an oven preheated to 425°F. Enjoy your delicious homemade buffalo chicken pizza served hot or cold! It's sure to become a family favorite.

Tuna Pizza

Ingredients

1 (8 ounce) package cream cheese, softened.
1 (14 ounce) package pre-baked pizza crust.
1 (5 ounce) can tuna, drained and flaked.
½ cup thinly sliced red onion.
1 ½ cups shredded mozzarella cheese.
crushed red pepper flakes, or to taste.

Tuna pizza is a delicious, easy-to-make recipe that will satisfy both seafood lovers and pizza enthusiasts. This delicious combination of cream cheese, tuna, red onion, and mozzarella cheese is sure to become one of your favorite delicious pizza recipes! To prepare this delicious treat, follow the steps below:

Firstly, preheat your oven to 375°F (190°C). Next, spread the softened cream cheese on the pre-baked pizza crust. Then add the flaked tuna, red onion slices, and shredded mozzarella cheese on top. Sprinkle some crushed red pepper flakes over the top according to taste. Finally, bake in preheated oven for 15 minutes or until cheese has melted and edges of crust are golden brown.

Enjoy your delicious tuna pizza! If you're looking for more delicious pizza recipes, be sure to check out our other delicious pizza recipes. Bon Appetit!

Napolitan Pizza

Ingredients

1 ball Best Homemade Pizza Dough.
⅓ cup Easy Pizza Sauce.
3 ounces fresh mozzarella cheese (or about ¾ cup shredded mozzarella)
Kosher salt.
2 basil leaves.
Semolina flour or cornmeal, for dusting the pizza peel.

Making delicious neapolitan pizza at home is easier than you think! All you need are a few simple ingredients and the right technique.

Start by preheating your oven to 500°F or higher. Place a pizza stone in the oven to heat up, as well. Next, prepare the dough. Roll out 1 ball of Best Homemade Pizza Dough on a lightly floured surface until it's about 10 inches in diameter. Transfer the dough onto a pizza peel dusted with semolina flour or cornmeal.
Spread ⅓ cup of Easy Pizza Sauce over the top of your crust and sprinkle with kosher salt. Add 3 ounces (or ¾ cup) of fresh mozzarella cheese and 2 basil leaves. Carefully slide the pizza off the peel onto the preheated pizza stone in the oven and bake for 3 to 10 minutes until golden brown.
Enjoy your delicious homemade neapolitan pizza! For more delicious pizza recipes, you can check out our website or visit us on social media. We look forward to hearing how you prepared this delicious meal! Bon Appétit!

Diavola Pizza

Diavola pizza is a delicious Italian dish that will tantalize your taste buds and make you come back for more. This delicious pizza recipe is made with Best Pizza Dough, Easy Pizza Sauce, fresh mozzarella cheese, Kalamata olives, Fresno or Calabrian chili pepper, and basil leaves. It's simple to prepare and can be ready in no time!

To begin making the diavola pizza, start by rolling out your chosen dough on a lightly floured surface into a 12-inch circle. Place the dough onto an oiled baking sheet or pizza stone. Spread ⅓ cup of homemade easy pizza sauce over the dough evenly leaving one inch around the edges. Top with 4 ounces of fresh mozzarella cheese and a sprinkle of kosher salt if desired. Add 8 to 10 Kalamata olives, one Fresno or Calabrian chili pepper, and two basil leaves to the top of the pizza.

Once all your delicious toppings are in place, bake at 475°F for about 18 minutes until the crust is golden brown and the cheese has melted and bubbled. Let cool for five minutes before serving warm. Enjoy!

Now that you have the recipe for this delicious diavola pizza, why not give it a try? The combination of flavors is sure to make this dish a favorite in your household. Serve with a delicious side salad or some garlic bread to complete the meal! Enjoy

Egg Pizza

Egg pizza is a delicious, easy to make snack that everyone can enjoy. It's full of flavor and the perfect treat for any occasion. To prepare egg pizza, you will need the following ingredients: 4 eggs, 1 medium onion, 3 thinly sliced cherry tomatoes, 1/2 cup finely chopped capsicum (green pepper), black pepper as required, 2 thinly sliced mushrooms, 1/2 cup grated cheese-cheddar and 1 tablespoon of refined oil.

First begin by preheating your oven to 375 degrees Fahrenheit. Then heat one tablespoon of oil in a pan over medium heat and add the onions. Cook until they start turning golden brown and then add the capsicum and mushroom slices. Cook for a few minutes and then add the eggs. Use a spatula to break the eggs and stir occasionally until they are cooked through and there is no visible liquid egg yolk.

Next, spread the mixture onto a greased baking pan. Top with thinly sliced cherry tomatoes, black pepper and grated cheese-cheddar. Bake in preheated oven for 15 minutes or until the cheese has melted and the pizza is lightly browned. Let it cool slightly before cutting into slices and serve hot with your favorite dip! Enjoy delicious Egg Pizza anytime you want!

This delicious recipe makes an excellent snack or light meal that can be easily prepared at home. With this simple guide, you will have delicious Egg Pizza in no time! Try out this delicious pizza recipe today and create delicious memories with your loved ones. Bon Appetit!

Mediterranean Pizza

Mediterranean pizza is a delicious and healthy way to enjoy pizza night. It's packed full of vegetables and delicious flavors that will leave you wanting more. The key to making the perfect Mediterranean pizza is picking the right ingredients. Here are some delicious options to try when making your own Mediterranean pizza:

- Hummus: This creamy dip gives an incredible flavor boost to any vegetarian dish, including pizzas. Spread hummus across the base of your pie before adding other toppings for a delicious twist on traditional tomato sauce.
- Green And Red Peppers: Bell peppers have an amazing crunchy texture that pairs perfectly with a cheese-filled crust or even under melted mozzarella cheese. For added color, contrast, and flavor, consider adding both green and red peppers to your Mediterranean pizza.
- Mushrooms: These delicious fungi are a great source of protein and, when cooked correctly, provide an earthy flavor that can't be beaten. Try adding mushrooms with some white cheese for an unbeatable combination.
- Zucchini: For added crunch and flavor, try grilling or sautéing zucchini before adding it to your pizza. The delicious veggie pairs perfectly with pesto, goat cheese, and other delicious flavors found in Mediterranean pizzas.
- Sun-Dried Tomatoes: These intensely flavored tomatoes add a sweet touch to any dish they are put into - including pizza! They go amazingly well with pesto and are a delicious addition to any Mediterranean pizza.

- Pesto: Pesto is a delicious Italian sauce that can be used as the base of any vegetarian dish, including pizzas. Add it with some mushrooms, zucchini, and sun-dried tomatoes for an unbeatable combination.
- Goat Cheese: This delicious cheese has a strong flavor that pairs perfectly with all the delicious ingredients found on Mediterranean pizzas. Try adding crumbled goat cheese over the top for added flavor.

When making your own Mediterranean pizza at home, there's no limit to what you can add or how delicious it can be! Feel free to experiment with different combinations of veggies, sauces and cheeses until you find your perfect pizza. Enjoy!

Mushroom Pizza

Ingredients

2 tablespoons olive oil.
2 tablespoons unsalted butter.
3 cloves garlic, minced.
16 ounces cremini mushrooms, thinly sliced.
½ teaspoon dried thyme.
½ teaspoon dried oregano.
Kosher salt and freshly ground black pepper, to taste.
¼ cup yellow cornmeal.

For delicious pizza recipes, this mushroom pizza is a must-try. To prepare it, start by preheating the oven to 375 degrees F (190 degrees C). Then heat the olive oil and butter in a large skillet over medium heat. Add garlic and mushrooms and cook until they are softened, about 5 minutes. Stir in thyme, oregano, salt and pepper.
Next, sprinkle some cornmeal onto a baking sheet or pizza pan. Spread the mushroom mixture evenly over the dough then bake for about 15 minutes or until the crust is lightly browned and crispy.
Serve your delicious mushroom pizza warm with your favorite toppings like cheese or fresh herbs!

Truffle Pizza

Truffle pizza is a delicious and unique way to enjoy pizza. To make this delicious pizza recipe, you'll need the following ingredients: 1 ball of Best Pizza Dough (or Food Processor Dough or Thin Crust Dough), 6 baby bella mushrooms (aka cremini), 1 garlic clove, 1 handful of chives, 1 tablespoon of olive oil plus more for drizzling, ¾ cup of shredded mozzarella cheese, and ¼ cup Parmesan cheese. In addition, you will need semolina flour or cornmeal to dust your pizza peel.

To prepare the truffle pizza first preheat oven to 425 degrees F. Roll out the dough on a lightly floured surface into desired shape. Place rolled-out dough onto a pizza peel or cookie sheet dusted with semolina flour or cornmeal.

Next, finely chop the mushrooms and garlic clove and add to a bowl with chives and olive oil. Mix together well. Spread this mixture evenly onto your prepared pizza dough, top with mozzarella cheese and Parmesan cheese. Place the pizza in preheated oven for about 8 minutes or until the crust is golden brown. Remove from oven, let cool slightly before slicing into desired pieces. Enjoy!

This delicious truffle pizza recipe is sure to be a hit with your family and friends! With just a few simple ingredients you can create an amazing delicious meal that everyone will love. Try this delicious truffle

Ricotta Pizza

If you're looking for delicious pizza recipes that won't take too long to prepare, look no further than ricotta pizza! This delicious meal combines the delicious flavors of ricotta cheese, mozzarella cheese, Parmesan cheese and artichoke hearts in a delicious combination. To make this delicious pizza, you'll need one ball of Best Pizza Dough (or Thin Crust Dough), ½ cup whole milk ricotta cheese, ⅛ teaspoon kosher salt to taste, fresh ground black pepper, ½ small garlic clove (¼ teaspoon minced), ½ cup shredded mozzarella cheese and ¼ cup shredded Parmesan cheese.

To begin the recipe, preheat your oven to 400°F. Roll out the dough into a 12-inch round and place on a baking sheet. Spread the ricotta cheese over the dough in an even layer, then sprinkle with salt and pepper to taste. Sprinkle the minced garlic, mozzarella cheese and artichoke hearts over the top of the pizza. Finally, sprinkle with Parmesan cheese and bake for 20-25 minutes or until golden brown. Enjoy!

This delicious ricotta pizza is sure to become a favorite in your house! It's quick and easy to prepare, yet delicious enough that everyone will enjoy it. Serve this delicious meal for dinner or as an appetizer at your next gathering—it won't disappoint!

Mexican Pizza

Ingredients

ground beef.
packet of taco seasoning (or homemade)
water.
oil.
corn tortillas.
refried beans.
red enchilada sauce.
shredded cheddar cheese.

Mexican Pizza is one of the delicious pizza recipes you can prepare in no time. It's a delicious, cheesy, and flavorful dish that everyone will love. Plus, it's so easy to make! Here's how to make Mexican Pizza:

1. Start by browning ground beef in a skillet over medium-high heat with some oil. Once cooked through, add taco seasoning mix and water according to package instructions and simmer for 5 minutes until thickened.
2. Spray or lightly brush both sides of corn tortillas with oil and place on baking sheet. Bake at 350 degrees for 10 minutes ("crisp up" the tortillas).
3. Spread refried beans over the "crisped up" tortillas. Top with cooked ground beef and sprinkle with shredded cheddar cheese.
4. Bake in preheated oven at 350 degrees for 15 minutes or until cheese is melted and bubbly.
5. Finally, top the Mexican Pizza with red enchilada sauce (or salsa) and any additional toppings of your choice such as onions, tomatoes, olives, jalapenos, etc. Serve immediately while hot! Enjoy!

Breakfast Pizza

1 pound ground breakfast sausage. Great Value Premium Original Ground Breakfast Sausage, 1 lb.
1 (8 ounce) package refrigerated crescent rolls.
1 cup frozen hash brown potatoes, thawed.
1 cup shredded Cheddar cheese.
5 eggs.
¼ cup milk.
½ teaspoon salt.
⅛ teaspoon ground black pepper.

This delicious pizza recipe is sure to become a favorite for breakfast! It's easy to prepare and all you need are a few simple ingredients. To make this delicious breakfast pizza, begin by preheating the oven to 375°F.

Next, in a large skillet over medium-high heat, cook the sausage until it is cooked through and beginning to brown. Drain off any excess fat from the cooked sausage before transferring it to an ungreased 12-inch pizza pan. Press the crescent roll dough onto the bottom of the pan and spread it out evenly with your fingertips or a spoon. Sprinkle on top of the sausage layer then spread out the hash brown potatoes evenly as well.

In a separate bowl, whisk together the eggs, milk, salt and pepper. Pour this mixture over the pizza ingredients in the pan and top with the shredded cheese. Bake for 25 minutes until golden brown. Let it cool slightly before serving.

With delicious sausage, hash browns and cheddar cheese, this breakfast pizza is sure to become a favorite! Enjoy it warm and savor this delicious recipe any time of day! This is definitely one of our go-to delicious pizza recipes. Have fun trying it out!

Pickle Pizza

Ingredients

1 recipe pizza dough (or store bought)
2 Tablespoons olive oil.
1 cup garlic pizza sauce.
4 cups shredded mozzarella cheese.
16 oz dill pickle slices, drained and patted dry.
dried or fresh dill, for garnish.

Pickle pizza is one of the delicious pizza recipes you can prepare at home. To make pickle pizza, start by preheating your oven to 400°F (204°C). Then, roll out the pizza dough on a greased baking sheet and brush it with olive oil. Spread the garlic pizza sauce over the dough and top it with shredded mozzarella cheese and dill pickle slices. Bake in preheated oven for 20 minutes or until golden brown. Sprinkle fresh or dried dill over the top before serving for extra flavor! Enjoy this unique and delicious twist on classic pizza!

Pickle pizza is sure to be a delicious hit with family and friends! With just a few simple ingredients, you can make an delicious homemade pickle pizza that everyone will love. Try this delicious recipe today and enjoy the unique flavor of pickles and cheese on your next pizza night!

Pesto Pizza

Are you looking for delicious pizza recipes? Making a pesto pizza is one of the best ways to enjoy a delicious and unique meal. With just a few simple ingredients, you can make this delicious homemade pizza in no time. Here's how to prepare it:

To start, preheat your oven to 425°F (220°C). Spread some cornmeal on your work surface and roll out the dough into desired size. Place the dough onto a baking sheet lined with parchment paper or lightly greased with olive oil.

Spread basil pesto over the dough using ½ cup of olive oil. Top with mozzarella cheese and roasted cherry tomatoes or sun-dried tomatoes. Bake in preheated oven until golden brown and bubbly, 18 to 20 minutes.

Once cooked, top with fresh basil and red pepper flakes for added flavor. Enjoy your delicious pesto pizza! It's a great addition to any meal or served as an appetizer. Bon appétit!

Cheese Shrimp Pizza

If you are looking for a delicious pizza recipe with shrimp, this is it! This delicious pizza combines the cheesy goodness of Gruyere and mozzarella cheeses along with delicious shrimp for an unbeatable combination. The dough is prepared and topped with a generous drizzle of olive oil before adding on the cheese, garlic, lemon zest, and parmesan cheese. Once cooked through in the oven, this delicious shrimp pizza will be ready to devour!

To prepare this delicious pizza, start by preheating your oven to 400°F while you prepare the dough. Roll out the dough into a 12-inch circle or rectangle if desired and place onto a greased baking sheet. Drizzle some of the olive oil onto the dough before topping with the Gruyere and mozzarella cheese. In a medium bowl, combine the shrimp, garlic, lemon zest and remaining olive oil. Mix together until completely combined then spread evenly onto the pizza dough. Sprinkle with parmesan cheese and bake in preheated oven for 25 minutes or until crust is golden brown and shrimp is cooked through.

Enjoy this delicious pizza recipe! The combination of cheeses, garlic, lemon zest, shrimp and parmesan cheese makes it irresistible! Enjoy your delicious shrimp pizza!

Focaccia Pizza

If you're looking for delicious pizza recipes, then look no further than focaccia pizza! This popular Italian dish is simple to prepare and full of delicious tastes. To get started, you'll need the following ingredients: 3 cups (15oz/422g) all-purpose flour, ½ teaspoon instant yeast, 2 teaspoons salt, 1 ⅓ cups (10 ½oz/282ml) water at room temperature, 2 tablespoons olive oil, ½ cup (4oz/115g) pizza sauce, 1 ½ cups (8oz/225g) mozzarella grated, and 10-12 pepperoni slices (optional).

To begin preparing this delicious dish, preheat your oven to 450°F. In a large bowl, mix together the flour, yeast, and salt. Once that's done, add in the water and olive oil and stir until a dough is formed. Knead it for 5 minutes on a lightly floured surface. Grease a 14-inch baking pan with olive oil before transferring your dough to it. Press the dough into the pan using your fingertips to form an even layer. Brush with additional oil if needed, then bake at 450°F for 12 minutes.

Once the crust has cooked through, remove from oven and spread pizza sauce over top followed by mozzarella and pepperoni (if desired). Bake again for 10-15 minutes or until cheese is melted and bubbling. Let cool slightly before cutting into slices and serving. Enjoy your delicious focaccia pizza!

You can also customize this delicious dish by adding any additional toppings of your choice! From mushrooms to bell peppers, the possibilities are endless. Give it a try and let us know how delicious your focaccia pizza turned out! Bon Appétit!

Goat Cheese Pizza

Goat Cheese Pizza is a delicious recipe that is both easy to make and delicious to eat. This delicious pizza combines delicious ingredients like homemade pizza sauce, mozzarella cheese, soft goat cheese, red onion slices and oregano into a delicious combination that will have your family coming back for seconds!

To start off this delicious meal, you will need one recipe of either the Best Pizza Dough, Thin Crust Pizza Dough or Pizza Oven Dough. Once you have the dough prepared, spread ⅓ cup of Homemade Pizza Sauce on top. Then sprinkle ½ cup of shredded mozzarella cheese over top. Break up 3 ounces of soft goat cheese (chevre) and dot it around the pizza. Lastly add 1 handful of red onion slices and a sprinkle of ¼ teaspoon dried oregano. Finish off the pizza by adding some kosher salt and fresh ground black pepper to taste.

Once all your delicious ingredients are added, bake in an oven preheated to 500°F for 10-15 minutes or until the cheese is melted and bubbly. For a delicious finishing touch, garnish with some fresh basil leaves before serving.

Try this delicious Goat Cheese Pizza recipe tonight and enjoy delicious, easy-to-make pizza that's sure to be a hit! Enjoy!

Veggie Pizza

If you're looking to make delicious veggie pizza, here's a delicious recipe that will get the job done. Start by preheating your oven to 425°F and preparing your ingredients. You'll need store-bought or homemade pizza sauce, vegan mozzarella cheese (optional), sliced red and green bell peppers, onions (white or yellow), mushrooms of your choice, olives (sliced black are traditional but other varieties like kalamata or castelvetrano can be delicious!), dried oregano, and fresh basil.

Instructions for assembling your pizza: spread the pizza sauce over a prepared crust and top with the cheese and veggies. Sprinkle with oregano before baking for 15-20 minutes or until the cheese is melted and the crust is golden. Finally, garnish with fresh basil before slicing and serving. Enjoy!

Creating delicious veggie pizza doesn't have to be complicated or time-consuming. With this simple recipe, you can make a delicious meal in no time. Whether it's for lunch, dinner, or a snack, you can rest assured that your pizza will be delicious every time! Bon appetit!

Basil Pizza

Ingredients

1 recipe Pizza Dough, stretched onto a 14-inch pizza pan or large baking sheet.
½ heaping cup Pizza Sauce.
8 ounces fresh mozzarella cheese, torn or sliced.
½ cup thinly sliced cherry tomatoes.
10 fresh basil leaves.
Pinch red pepper flakes.
Extra-virgin olive oil, for drizzling.

This delicious homemade basil pizza is sure to be a hit with your family and friends. Start by preheating the oven to 450°F (232°C). Then, stretch out one recipe of Pizza Dough onto a 14-inch pizza pan or large baking sheet. Spread ½ heaping cup of Pizza Sauce over the dough, followed by 8 ounces of torn or sliced fresh mozzarella cheese, ½ cup thinly sliced cherry tomatoes, 10 fresh basil leaves, and a pinch of red pepper flakes. Drizzle lightly with extra-virgin olive oil before baking in the preheated oven for 17-20 minutes until golden brown. Serve hot as an appetizer or main course! This delicious basil pizza recipe is sure to become one of your go-to delicious pizza recipes. Enjoy!

Pan Pizza

Making delicious pan pizza is easier than you think with the right ingredients. To make your own delicious pan pizza, start by combining 2 1/4 cups of all-purpose flour and 1 teaspoon of kosher salt in a large bowl. Sprinkle in 3/4 teaspoon of active dry yeast, then add 3/4 cup plus 3 tablespoons of lukewarm water and mix until the dough comes together. Knead the dough on a lightly floured surface for about 5 minutes until it is smooth and elastic. Transfer the dough to an oiled bowl, cover with plastic wrap, and let rise for at least one hour.

Meanwhile, prepare the toppings by mashing two cloves of garlic with one tablespoon olive oil until it forms a paste. Spread one tablespoon of olive oil over the bottom of a greased 10-inch skillet, then roll out the dough in the pan until it covers the base. Spread the garlic paste and tomato sauce over the dough, sprinkle with some dried oregano, and bake for 18 to 20 minutes at 400°F. Enjoy your delicious pizza hot from the oven!

Making delicious pan pizza does not have to be complicated - all you need is some simple ingredients and a few steps to get started. With just a little patience and practice, you can create delicious pizzas that will impress anyone! Try experimenting with different toppings or flavor combinations to make new delicious recipes each time. So what are you waiting for? Get making delicious pizza in no time!

Happy cooking!

White Pizza

White pizza is a delicious and unique alternative to the traditional red sauce-topped pizzas. This delicious, garlicky white pizza recipe is sure to be a hit! Prepared with the right ingredients, it can make for a delicious lunch or dinner dish.

To prepare this delicious white pizza, you will need: dough for one large pizza, two tablespoons of olive oil, three minced garlic cloves, eight ounces ball fresh mozzarella sliced thinly, 1/3 cup ricotta cheese, 1/2 teaspoon kosher salt, 1/4 teaspoon freshly ground black pepper, 1/8 teaspoon dried oregano, 1/8 teaspoon dried thyme and 1/3 cup freshly grated Pecorino Romano or Parmesan cheese.

Start by preheating your oven to 375°F and lightly greasing a large, rimmed baking sheet. Unroll the pizza dough onto the pan and press it out into an even thickness. Then, brush the olive oil over the surface of the dough and sprinkle with minced garlic cloves. Layer thinly-sliced mozzarella over top of the garlic and drizzle with ricotta cheese. Sprinkle with salt, pepper, oregano and thyme. Finally, top everything off with freshly grated Pecorino Romano or Parmesan cheese.

Place in preheated oven and bake for 15 to 20 minutes until the crust is golden brown and delicious! Serve hot and enjoy!

This delicious white pizza is sure to be a hit with the whole family. With its garlicky flavor and delicious cheese-topped crust, it makes for a delicious lunch or dinner dish. So why not give this delicious recipe a try tonight? You won't regret it!

Spinach And Ricotta Pizza

Ingredients

1 batch rustic pizza dough.
1 lb ricotta cheese.
1 lb fontina cheese shredded.
1/4 c parmigiano reggianno grated.
1 1/2 lb garlic spinach.
20 cloves garlic.
pinch of sea salt.
black pepper to taste freshly cracked.

This delicious spinach and ricotta pizza recipe is easy to make and sure to please the whole family. To start, prepare a batch of rustic pizza dough and preheat your oven to 500°F. Once the oven is up to temperature, spread out the pizza dough into a large round shape on an oiled baking sheet or pan.

Next, combine the ricotta cheese, fontina cheese, parmigiano reggianno and garlic together in a bowl until fully combined. Spread this mixture evenly over the pizza dough and top with spinach leaves. Finally, sprinkle some sea salt and freshly cracked black pepper over the pizza before transferring it into the oven for 10-12 minutes or until golden brown and crispy on the edges.

Enjoy your delicious spinach and ricotta pizza straight from the oven for a delicious dinner or lunch. With just a few pre-prepared ingredients, you can have restaurant quality pizza at home in no time. Be sure to share this delicious recipe with your friends and family, they'll love it as much as you do! Bon Appetit!

Spinach And Feta Pizza

Ingredients

2 large Pizza Bases (see notes)
½ cup Tomato Paste.
½ Brown / Yellow Onion, finely diced.
½ Red Capsicum / Bell Pepper, finely diced.
100g / 3.5 oz Baby Spinach, roughly chopped.
4 White Mushrooms, thinly sliced.
½ cup Feta Cheese, crumbled.
1 ½ cups Shredded Mozzarella Cheese (or more, to taste)

Making delicious spinach and feta pizzas is easy and delicious. To begin, preheat your oven to 200°C / 392°F. Place the pizza bases on a lightly greased baking tray. Spread a thin layer of tomato paste over each base, then scatter the diced onion, capsicum / bell pepper, mushrooms, baby spinach and crumbled feta cheese over the top. Sprinkle with mozzarella cheese (you can add more if desired). Bake for 15-20 minutes or until golden brown and bubbly. Serve hot! Enjoy your delicious spinach and feta pizza!

These delicious spinach and feta pizzas are sure to become a family favorite in no time! The combination of flavors from the vegetables, feta and mozzarella cheese makes for a delicious meal that is sure to please everyone. With just a few simple ingredients, you can easily make delicious pizza recipes at home with ease! No need to order take-out anymore - now you can make delicious pizzas right in your own kitchen. Enjoy!

Spinach Alfredo Pizza

Ingredients

1 13 oz puff pastry sheet.
½ cup Alfredo sauce any jar or type will work.
12 oz. marinated artichoke hearts chopped.
1 cup fresh spinach leaves.
2 Tbsp. green onions chopped.
8 oz. log mozzarella cheese sliced.
½ cup parmesan cheese shredded.
1 Tbsp. Everything Bagel seasoning ad.!

This delicious Spinach Alfredo Pizza is a great way to enjoy a delicious pizza without having to order from your favorite pizzeria. With its delicious combination of Alfredo sauce, artichoke hearts, spinach, and mozzarella cheese, this pizza will be sure to satisfy even the pickiest of eaters.

To prepare this delicious pizza, start by preheating your oven to 375 degrees Fahrenheit. Then unroll the puff pastry sheet onto a greased baking sheet or round stone. Spread the Alfredo sauce over the entire sheet until evenly covered and sprinkle with chopped artichoke hearts, fresh spinach leaves and green onions. Top with sliced mozzarella cheese and shredded parmesan cheese before sprinkling with everything bagel seasoning.

Bake in your preheated oven for 25-30 minutes or until the cheese is golden and bubbly. Let cool slightly before serving and enjoy!

This delicious Spinach Alfredo Pizza is one of many delicious pizza recipes you can make at home and it's sure to be a hit with everyone in the family. Give this delicious pizza recipe a try today and let us know how it turns out! Enjoy!

Arugula Pizza

INGREDIENTS

1 ¼ cup pizza sauce (purchased or our favorite Easy Pizza Sauce)
1 cup (3 ounces) shredded smoked gouda cheese.
½ cup shredded Parmesan cheese.
6 ounces fresh mozzarella cheese.
4 cups (3 ounces) baby arugula.
1 tablespoon extra virgin olive oil.
¼ teaspoon kosher salt, plus more for sprinkling.

If you're looking for delicious pizza recipes, look no further than this delicious arugula pizza. This delicious and easy-to-prepare meal is perfect for any day of the week. To make it, start by preheating your oven to 500°F (260°C). Next, spread 1 ¼ cups of purchased or homemade pizza sauce on a 12 inch baking sheet lined with parchment paper. Top with 1 cup (3 ounces) shredded smoked gouda cheese, ½ cup shredded Parmesan cheese, and 6 ounces fresh mozzarella cheese. Bake in the preheated oven for 10 minutes until golden brown and bubbly. Once done baking, top the pizza with 4 cups (3 ounces) baby arugula and sprinkle with 1 tablespoon extra virgin olive oil and ¼ teaspoon kosher salt. Slice, serve, and enjoy! With its delicious combination of flavors, this delicious arugula pizza is sure to become a family favorite. Enjoy!

Cheese Pizza

Are you craving delicious pizza but don't know how to prepare one? Look no further, as we have the perfect cheese pizza recipe for you! To make this delicious meal, you will need 1/2 recipe of homemade pizza crust, 1/2-3/4 cup (127-190g) of your favorite pizza sauce (homemade or store-bought), 8 ounces of sliced mozzarella cheese, 1 and 1/2 cups (6oz or 168g) shredded mozzarella cheese, 2-3 Tablespoons (10-15g) grated Parmesan cheese, and dried basil or Italian seasoning.

To begin, preheat your oven to 425°F (218°C). Then spread out the pizza dough on a baking sheet or pizza pan. Next, spread the sauce over the pizza crust, then top with sliced and shredded mozzarella cheese. Sprinkle parmesan cheese and dried basil/Italian seasoning over the top of the pizza. Bake for 12-15 minutes until the cheese is melted and golden brown. Let cool slightly before cutting into slices to serve. Enjoy your delicious homemade cheese pizza!

With a few simple ingredients, you can enjoy delicious homemade cheese pizza in no time! So what are you waiting for? Try out this delicious recipe today!

Best Ever Sheet Pan Pizza

Ingredients:

For the pizza dough:

4 cups all-purpose flour
2 ¼ teaspoons instant yeast
2 teaspoons sugar
2 teaspoons salt
1 ½ cups warm water
2 tablespoons olive oil

Instructions:

In a small bowl, combine warm water, sugar, and instant yeast. Stir gently and let it sit for about 5 minutes until the mixture becomes frothy.
In a large mixing bowl, combine the flour and salt. Make a well in the center and pour in the yeast mixture and olive oil. Stir everything together until a dough forms.
Transfer the dough onto a lightly floured surface and knead for about 5-7 minutes until the dough becomes smooth and elastic. If the dough is too sticky, add a little more flour.
Place the dough in a greased bowl and cover it with a clean kitchen towel. Allow it to rise in a warm place for about 1-2 hours or until it doubles in size.
Preheat your oven to 475°F (245°C). Place a sheet pan (18x13 inches) in the oven while it preheats.
Once the dough has risen, punch it down and transfer it to a lightly floured surface. Divide the dough in half.
Roll out one portion of the dough into a rectangle slightly larger than the size of the sheet pan.
Carefully remove the hot sheet pan from the oven and drizzle it with a little olive oil. Carefully transfer the rolled-out dough onto the hot sheet pan.
Gently stretch and press the dough to fit the pan evenly, making sure it reaches the edges.
Spread half of the pizza sauce evenly over the dough, leaving a small border around the edges.
Sprinkle half of the shredded mozzarella cheese evenly over the sauce.
Add your desired pizza toppings over the cheese.
Repeat steps 7-12 with the remaining dough and toppings.
Place the sheet pan in the preheated oven and bake for about 15-20 minutes, or until the crust is golden brown and the cheese is melted and bubbly.
Remove the sheet pan from the oven and let it cool for a few minutes. Sprinkle with fresh basil leaves, grated Parmesan cheese, and red pepper flakes if desired.
Slice the Best-Ever Sheet Pan Pizza into squares and serve it hot.
Enjoy your delicious homemade Sheet Pan Pizza!

Everything Basil Pizza

Ingredients:

For the pizza dough:

2 ½ cups all-purpose flour
1 teaspoon instant yeast
1 teaspoon sugar
1 teaspoon salt
1 cup warm water
2 tablespoons olive oil

For the pizza toppings:

½ cup tomato sauce or marinara sauce
2 cups shredded mozzarella cheese
¼ cup grated Parmesan cheese
2 tablespoons sesame seeds
2 tablespoons poppy seeds
2 tablespoons dried minced onion
2 tablespoons dried minced garlic
2 tablespoons dried basil
Fresh basil leaves, torn
Red pepper flakes (optional)

Instructions:

In a small bowl, combine warm water, sugar, and instant yeast. Stir gently and let it sit for about 5 minutes until the mixture becomes frothy.
In a large mixing bowl, combine the flour and salt. Make a well in the center and pour in the yeast mixture and olive oil. Stir everything together until a dough forms.
Transfer the dough onto a lightly floured surface and knead for about 5-7 minutes until the dough becomes smooth and elastic. If the dough is too sticky, add a little more flour.
Place the dough in a greased bowl and cover it with a clean kitchen towel. Allow it to rise in a warm place for about 1 hour or until it doubles in size.
Preheat your oven to 475°F (245°C). If you have a pizza stone, place it in the oven while it preheats.
Once the dough has risen, punch it down and roll it out on a lightly floured surface into your desired pizza shape.
Transfer the rolled-out dough onto a baking sheet or a pizza peel if using a pizza stone.
Spread the tomato sauce evenly over the pizza dough, leaving a small border around the edges.
Sprinkle the shredded mozzarella cheese and grated Parmesan cheese over the sauce.
In a small bowl, mix together the sesame seeds, poppy seeds, dried minced onion, dried minced garlic, and dried basil. Sprinkle this mixture evenly over the cheese.
Place the pizza in the preheated oven and bake for about 15-20 minutes, or until the crust is golden brown and the cheese is melted and bubbly.
Remove the pizza from the oven and let it cool for a minute. Sprinkle torn fresh basil leaves over the top. Add a sprinkle of red pepper flakes if desired.
Drizzle the pizza with olive oil and let it rest for a few minutes.
Slice the Everything Basil Pizza and serve it hot.
Enjoy your delicious Everything Basil Pizza with a unique blend of flavors and textures!

Homemade Supreme Pizza

Ingredients:

For the dough:

2 ¼ cups all-purpose flour
1 teaspoon instant yeast
1 teaspoon sugar
1 teaspoon salt
1 cup warm water

For the pizza toppings:
½ cup pizza sauce
2 cups shredded mozzarella cheese
¼ cup sliced pepperoni
¼ cup sliced black olives
¼ cup sliced green bell pepper
¼ cup sliced red onion
¼ cup sliced mushrooms
¼ cup sliced Italian sausage
1 teaspoon dried oregano
1 teaspoon dried basil
Salt and pepper to taste

Instructions:

In a large mixing bowl, combine the flour, instant yeast, sugar, and salt. Mix well.
Add the warm water and olive oil to the bowl. Stir until the ingredients are well combined and form a dough.
Transfer the dough onto a floured surface and knead for about 5 minutes until it becomes smooth and elastic. If the dough is too sticky, you can add a little more flour.
Place the dough in a greased bowl and cover it with a damp cloth. Allow it to rise in a warm place for about 1 to 1.5 hours or until it doubles in size.
Preheat your oven to 475°F (245°C) and place a pizza stone or baking sheet in the oven to heat up.
Punch down the risen dough and divide it into two equal portions. Roll out each portion into a round shape to your desired thickness.
Carefully transfer one of the dough rounds onto a sheet of parchment paper or a pizza peel dusted with flour or cornmeal.
Spread half of the pizza sauce evenly over the dough, leaving a small border around the edges for the crust.
Sprinkle half of the shredded mozzarella cheese over the sauce.
Arrange the pepperoni, black olives, green bell pepper, red onion, mushrooms, and Italian sausage over the cheese.
Sprinkle dried oregano, dried basil, salt, and pepper over the toppings.
Carefully transfer the pizza (with the parchment paper or pizza peel) onto the preheated baking sheet or pizza stone in the oven.
Bake for about 12-15 minutes, or until the crust is golden brown and the cheese is bubbly and slightly browned.
Remove the pizza from the oven and let it cool for a few minutes before slicing and serving.
Repeat the process with the second dough round and remaining toppings.
Enjoy your homemade Supreme Pizza!

Bacon Breakfast Pizza

Ingredients:

For the pizza dough:

2 ¼ cups all-purpose flour
1 teaspoon instant yeast
1 teaspoon sugar
1 teaspoon salt
1 cup warm water
2 tablespoons olive oil

For the pizza toppings:

½ cup breakfast sausage, cooked and crumbled
4 slices bacon, cooked and crumbled
4 large eggs
½ cup shredded cheddar cheese
½ cup shredded mozzarella cheese
Salt and pepper to taste
Chopped green onions or parsley for garnish
(optional)

Instructions:

In a large mixing bowl, combine the flour, instant yeast, sugar, and salt. Mix well.
Add the warm water and olive oil to the bowl. Stir until the ingredients are well combined and form a dough.
Transfer the dough onto a floured surface and knead for about 5 minutes until it becomes smooth and elastic. If the dough is too sticky, you can add a little more flour.
Place the dough in a greased bowl and cover it with a damp cloth. Allow it to rise in a warm place for about 1 to 1.5 hours or until it doubles in size.
Preheat your oven to 475°F (245°C) and place a pizza stone or baking sheet in the oven to heat up.
Cook the bacon in a skillet over medium heat until crispy. Remove from the skillet and crumble it into small pieces.
In the same skillet, cook the breakfast sausage until browned and cooked through. Remove from the skillet and crumble it as well.
Roll out the risen dough into a round shape to your desired thickness. Carefully transfer it onto a sheet of parchment paper or a pizza peel dusted with flour or cornmeal.
Spread the shredded mozzarella cheese evenly over the dough, leaving a small border around the edges for the crust.
Sprinkle the crumbled bacon and breakfast sausage over the cheese.
Create four small wells on the pizza, evenly spaced apart. Crack an egg into each well.
Season the eggs with salt and pepper to taste.
Carefully transfer the pizza (with the parchment paper or pizza peel) onto the preheated baking sheet or pizza stone in the oven.
Bake for about 12-15 minutes, or until the crust is golden brown and the eggs are cooked to your desired level of doneness.
Remove the pizza from the oven and let it cool for a few minutes. Sprinkle the shredded cheddar cheese over the top and garnish with chopped green onions or parsley if desired.
Slice and serve the Bacon Breakfast Pizza while it's still warm.
Enjoy your delicious Bacon Breakfast Pizza!

Pepperoni Pizza

Ingredients:

For the pizza dough:

2 ¼ cups all-purpose flour
1 teaspoon instant yeast
1 teaspoon sugar
1 teaspoon salt
1 cup warm water
2 tablespoons olive oil

For the pizza toppings:

½ cup pizza sauce
2 cups shredded mozzarella cheese
40-50 slices of pepperoni
1 teaspoon dried oregano
1 teaspoon dried basil
Salt and pepper to taste

Instructions:

In a large mixing bowl, combine the flour, instant yeast, sugar, and salt. Mix well.
Add the warm water and olive oil to the bowl. Stir until the ingredients are well combined and form a dough.
Transfer the dough onto a floured surface and knead for about 5 minutes until it becomes smooth and elastic. If the dough is too sticky, you can add a little more flour.
Place the dough in a greased bowl and cover it with a damp cloth. Allow it to rise in a warm place for about 1 to 1.5 hours or until it doubles in size.
Preheat your oven to 475°F (245°C) and place a pizza stone or baking sheet in the oven to heat up.
Roll out the risen dough into a round shape to your desired thickness. Carefully transfer it onto a sheet of parchment paper or a pizza peel dusted with flour or cornmeal.
Spread the pizza sauce evenly over the dough, leaving a small border around the edges for the crust.
Sprinkle the shredded mozzarella cheese over the sauce, covering the entire surface.
Arrange the pepperoni slices over the cheese. You can place them in a single layer or slightly overlap them.
Sprinkle dried oregano, dried basil, salt, and pepper over the toppings.
Carefully transfer the pizza (with the parchment paper or pizza peel) onto the preheated baking sheet or pizza stone in the oven.
Bake for about 12-15 minutes, or until the crust is golden brown and the cheese is bubbly and slightly browned.
Remove the pizza from the oven and let it cool for a few minutes before slicing and serving.

BBQ Chicken Pizza

Ingredients:
For the pizza dough:

2 ¼ cups all-purpose flour
1 teaspoon instant yeast
1 teaspoon sugar
1 teaspoon salt
1 cup warm water
2 tablespoons olive oil

For the pizza toppings:

½ cup barbecue sauce
2 cups cooked chicken breast, shredded or diced
1 cup shredded mozzarella cheese
½ cup red onion, thinly sliced
¼ cup chopped fresh cilantro (optional)
Salt and pepper to taste

Instructions:

In a large mixing bowl, combine the flour, instant yeast, sugar, and salt. Mix well.
Add the warm water and olive oil to the bowl. Stir until the ingredients are well combined and form a dough.
Transfer the dough onto a floured surface and knead for about 5 minutes until it becomes smooth and elastic. If the dough is too sticky, you can add a little more flour.
Place the dough in a greased bowl and cover it with a damp cloth. Allow it to rise in a warm place for about 1 to 1.5 hours or until it doubles in size.
Preheat your oven to 475°F (245°C) and place a pizza stone or baking sheet in the oven to heat up.
Roll out the risen dough into a round shape to your desired thickness. Carefully transfer it onto a sheet of parchment paper or a pizza peel dusted with flour or cornmeal.
Spread the barbecue sauce evenly over the dough, leaving a small border around the edges for the crust.
Sprinkle the shredded mozzarella cheese over the sauce, covering the entire surface.
Distribute the cooked chicken breast evenly over the cheese.
Scatter the thinly sliced red onion on top.
Season with salt and pepper to taste.
Carefully transfer the pizza (with the parchment paper or pizza peel) onto the preheated baking sheet or pizza stone in the oven.
Bake for about 12-15 minutes, or until the crust is golden brown and the cheese is bubbly and slightly browned.
Remove the pizza from the oven and let it cool for a few minutes. Sprinkle chopped fresh cilantro over the top if desired.
Slice and serve the BBQ Chicken Pizza while it's still warm.
Enjoy your delicious BBQ Chicken Pizza!

Easy Grilled Pizza

Ingredients:

For the pizza dough:
2 ¼ cups all-purpose flour
1 teaspoon instant yeast
1 teaspoon sugar
1 teaspoon salt
1 cup warm water
2 tablespoons olive oil

For the pizza toppings:

½ cup pizza sauce
2 cups shredded mozzarella cheese
Your choice of toppings (e.g., sliced pepperoni, sliced bell peppers, sliced onions, mushrooms, etc.)
Fresh basil leaves (optional)
Salt and pepper to taste

Instructions:

In a large mixing bowl, combine the flour, instant yeast, sugar, and salt. Mix well.
Add the warm water and olive oil to the bowl. Stir until the ingredients are well combined and form a dough.
Transfer the dough onto a floured surface and knead for about 5 minutes until it becomes smooth and elastic. If the dough is too sticky, you can add a little more flour.
Place the dough in a greased bowl and cover it with a damp cloth. Allow it to rise in a warm place for about 1 to 1.5 hours or until it doubles in size.
Preheat your grill to medium-high heat.
Divide the risen dough into desired portions. Roll out each portion into a round shape to your desired thickness.
Place the rolled-out dough onto a sheet of parchment paper.
Carefully transfer the dough (with the parchment paper) onto the preheated grill grates. Close the lid and cook for about 2-3 minutes, or until the bottom is lightly charred and the dough is set.
Using a pair of tongs or a spatula, flip the dough over.
Spread the pizza sauce evenly over the grilled side of the dough, leaving a small border around the edges for the crust.
Sprinkle the shredded mozzarella cheese over the sauce, covering the entire surface.
Add your choice of toppings (e.g., pepperoni, bell peppers, onions, mushrooms, etc.) on top of the cheese.
Sprinkle with salt and pepper to taste.
Close the grill lid and cook for an additional 4-6 minutes, or until the cheese is melted and bubbly, and the bottom of the crust is cooked through.
Remove the grilled pizza from the grill using the tongs or spatula. Let it cool for a minute or two.
Optional: Garnish with fresh basil leaves.
Slice and serve the Easy Grilled Pizza while it's still warm.
Enjoy your delicious Easy Grilled Pizza!

Smoked Salmon Pizza

Ingredients:

For the pizza dough:
2 ¼ cups all-purpose flour
1 teaspoon instant yeast
1 teaspoon sugar
1 teaspoon salt
1 cup warm water
2 tablespoons olive oil

For the pizza toppings:

4 ounces cream cheese, softened
2 tablespoons fresh dill, chopped
1 tablespoon lemon juice
½ cup red onion, thinly sliced
4 ounces smoked salmon, thinly sliced
2 tablespoons capers
Freshly ground black pepper
Fresh arugula or mixed greens (optional)

Instructions:

In a large mixing bowl, combine the flour, instant yeast, sugar, and salt. Mix well.
Add the warm water and olive oil to the bowl. Stir until the ingredients are well combined and form a dough.
Transfer the dough onto a floured surface and knead for about 5 minutes until it becomes smooth and elastic. If the dough is too sticky, you can add a little more flour.
Place the dough in a greased bowl and cover it with a damp cloth. Allow it to rise in a warm place for about 1 to 1.5 hours or until it doubles in size.
Preheat your oven to 475°F (245°C) and place a pizza stone or baking sheet in the oven to heat up.
In a small bowl, combine the softened cream cheese, fresh dill, and lemon juice. Mix until well combined.
Roll out the risen dough into a round shape to your desired thickness. Carefully transfer it onto a sheet of parchment paper or a pizza peel dusted with flour or cornmeal.
Spread the cream cheese mixture evenly over the dough, leaving a small border around the edges for the crust.
Scatter the thinly sliced red onion on top of the cream cheese mixture.
Arrange the smoked salmon slices over the onions.
Sprinkle the capers over the salmon.
Grind some freshly ground black pepper over the top.
Carefully transfer the pizza (with the parchment paper or pizza peel) onto the preheated baking sheet or pizza stone in the oven.
Bake for about 12-15 minutes, or until the crust is golden brown.
Remove the pizza from the oven and let it cool for a few minutes. Top with fresh arugula or mixed greens if desired.
Slice and serve the Smoked Salmon Pizza while it's still warm.
Enjoy your delicious Smoked Salmon Pizza!

Roasted Garlic, Chicken and Spinach White Pizza

Ingredients:
- For the roasted garlic:
1 whole garlic bulb
1 tablespoon olive oil
Salt and pepper to taste

For the pizza dough:
2 ¼ cups all-purpose flour
1 teaspoon instant yeast
1 teaspoon sugar
1 teaspoon salt
1 cup warm water
2 tablespoons olive oil

For the pizza toppings:

1 cup ricotta cheese
2 cups shredded mozzarella cheese
1 cup cooked chicken breast, shredded or diced
2 cups fresh spinach leaves
1 tablespoon fresh basil, chopped
Red pepper flakes (optional)
Salt and pepper to taste

Instructions:

Preheat your oven to 400°F (200°C).

Cut off the top of the garlic bulb to expose the cloves. Place it on a piece of aluminum foil.
Drizzle olive oil over the exposed cloves and sprinkle with salt and pepper. Wrap the garlic bulb tightly in the foil.
Place the wrapped garlic bulb in the preheated oven and roast for about 30-35 minutes, or until the cloves are soft and golden brown. Remove from the oven and let it cool. Once cooled, squeeze the roasted garlic cloves out of the skin and set aside.
In a large mixing bowl, combine the flour, instant yeast, sugar, and salt for the pizza dough. Mix well.
Add the warm water and olive oil to the bowl. Stir until the ingredients are well combined and form a dough.
Transfer the dough onto a floured surface and knead for about 5 minutes until it becomes smooth and elastic. If the dough is too sticky, you can add a little more flour.
Place the dough in a greased bowl and cover it with a damp cloth. Allow it to rise in a warm place for about 1 to 1.5 hours or until it doubles in size.
Preheat your oven to 475°F (245°C) and place a pizza stone or baking sheet in the oven to heat up.
Roll out the risen dough into a round shape to your desired thickness. Carefully transfer it onto a sheet of parchment paper or a pizza peel dusted with flour or cornmeal.
In a small bowl, combine the ricotta cheese and roasted garlic cloves. Mix until well combined.
Spread the ricotta and roasted garlic mixture evenly over the dough, leaving a small border around the edges for the crust.
Sprinkle the shredded mozzarella cheese over the ricotta mixture, covering the entire surface.
Distribute the cooked chicken breast and fresh spinach leaves evenly on top of the cheese.
Sprinkle the fresh basil over the toppings. If desired, add red pepper flakes for some heat. Season with salt and pepper to taste.
Carefully transfer the pizza (with the parchment paper or pizza peel) onto the preheated baking sheet or pizza stone in the oven.
Bake for about 12-15 minutes, or until the crust is golden brown and the cheese is bubbly and slightly browned.

Meat Lovers Pizza

Ingredients:

For the pizza dough:
2 ¼ cups all-purpose flour
1 teaspoon instant yeast
1 teaspoon sugar
1 teaspoon salt
1 cup warm water
2 tablespoons olive oil

For the pizza toppings:

½ cup pizza sauce
2 cups shredded mozzarella cheese
½ cup cooked and crumbled bacon
½ cup cooked and crumbled Italian sausage
½ cup sliced pepperoni
½ cup sliced ham
½ cup sliced cooked chicken or ground beef (optional)
1 teaspoon dried oregano

Instructions:

In a large mixing bowl, combine the flour, instant yeast, sugar, and salt. Mix well.
Add the warm water and olive oil to the bowl. Stir until the ingredients are well combined and form a dough.
Transfer the dough onto a floured surface and knead for about 5 minutes until it becomes smooth and elastic. If the dough is too sticky, you can add a little more flour.
Place the dough in a greased bowl and cover it with a damp cloth. Allow it to rise in a warm place for about 1 to 1.5 hours or until it doubles in size.
Preheat your oven to 475°F (245°C) and place a pizza stone or baking sheet in the oven to heat up.
Roll out the risen dough into a round shape to your desired thickness. Carefully transfer it onto a sheet of parchment paper or a pizza peel dusted with flour or cornmeal.
Spread the pizza sauce evenly over the dough, leaving a small border around the edges for the crust.
Sprinkle the shredded mozzarella cheese over the sauce, covering the entire surface.
Distribute the cooked and crumbled bacon, Italian sausage, sliced pepperoni, sliced ham, and any other desired meats evenly over the cheese.
If using cooked chicken or ground beef, distribute it over the other meats.
Sprinkle dried oregano over the toppings. Season with salt and pepper to taste.
Carefully transfer the pizza (with the parchment paper or pizza peel) onto the preheated baking sheet or pizza stone in the oven.
Bake for about 12-15 minutes, or until the crust is golden brown and the cheese is bubbly and slightly browned.
Remove the pizza from the oven and let it cool for a few minutes before slicing and serving.
Enjoy your delicious Meat Lovers Pizza, packed with all the savory meats you love!

Chicken Pesto Pizza

Ingredients:

For the pizza dough:
2 ¼ cups all-purpose flour
1 teaspoon instant yeast
1 teaspoon sugar
1 teaspoon salt
1 cup warm water
2 tablespoons olive oil

For the pizza toppings:

½ cup basil pesto
2 cups shredded mozzarella cheese
1 cup cooked chicken breast, shredded or diced
½ cup cherry tomatoes, halved
¼ cup red onion, thinly sliced
¼ cup sliced black olives (optional)
Fresh basil leaves, for garnish
Salt and pepper to taste

Instructions:

In a large mixing bowl, combine the flour, instant yeast, sugar, and salt. Mix well.
Add the warm water and olive oil to the bowl. Stir until the ingredients are well combined and form a dough.
Transfer the dough onto a floured surface and knead for about 5 minutes until it becomes smooth and elastic. If the dough is too sticky, you can add a little more flour.
Place the dough in a greased bowl and cover it with a damp cloth. Allow it to rise in a warm place for about 1 to 1.5 hours or until it doubles in size.
Preheat your oven to 475°F (245°C) and place a pizza stone or baking sheet in the oven to heat up.
Roll out the risen dough into a round shape to your desired thickness. Carefully transfer it onto a sheet of parchment paper or a pizza peel dusted with flour or cornmeal.
Spread the basil pesto evenly over the dough, leaving a small border around the edges for the crust.
Sprinkle the shredded mozzarella cheese over the pesto, covering the entire surface.
Distribute the cooked chicken breast, cherry tomatoes, red onion, and sliced black olives (if using) evenly over the cheese.
Season with salt and pepper to taste.
Carefully transfer the pizza (with the parchment paper or pizza peel) onto the preheated baking sheet or pizza stone in the oven.
Bake for about 12-15 minutes, or until the crust is golden brown and the cheese is bubbly and slightly browned.
Remove the pizza from the oven and let it cool for a few minutes. Garnish with fresh basil leaves.
Slice and serve the Chicken Pesto Pizza while it's still warm.
Enjoy your delicious Chicken Pesto Pizza, filled with the flavors of basil pesto and tender chicken!

Chicago Style Deep Dish Pizza Recipe

For the pizza dough:

3 ¼ cups all-purpose flour
1 teaspoon sugar
1 teaspoon salt
2 ¼ teaspoons instant yeast
1 ¼ cups warm water
2 tablespoons olive oil

For the pizza filling:

1 pound Italian sausage, crumbled and cooked
1 ½ cups shredded mozzarella cheese
1 ½ cups shredded provolone cheese
1 cup pizza sauce
1 green bell pepper, sliced
1 small onion, sliced
1 cup sliced mushrooms
¼ cup grated Parmesan cheese
1 teaspoon dried oregano
1 teaspoon dried basil
½ teaspoon garlic powder
Salt and pepper to taste

Instructions:

In a large mixing bowl, combine the flour, sugar, salt, and instant yeast. Mix well.
Add the warm water and olive oil to the bowl. Stir until the ingredients are well combined and form a dough.
Transfer the dough onto a floured surface and knead for about 5 minutes until it becomes smooth and elastic. If the dough is too sticky, you can add a little more flour.
Place the dough in a greased bowl and cover it with a damp cloth. Allow it to rise in a warm place for about 1 to 1.5 hours or until it doubles in size.
Preheat your oven to 425°F (220°C).
Punch down the risen dough and transfer it to a deep-dish pizza pan or a round cake pan greased with olive oil. Press the dough evenly across the bottom and up the sides of the pan, forming a crust.
Layer the cooked Italian sausage, shredded mozzarella cheese, and shredded provolone cheese in the crust.
Spread the pizza sauce over the cheese and sausage.
Arrange the sliced green bell pepper, onion, and mushrooms on top of the sauce.
In a small bowl, combine the grated Parmesan cheese, dried oregano, dried basil, garlic powder, salt, and pepper. Sprinkle this mixture evenly over the toppings.
Place the pizza in the preheated oven and bake for about 30-35 minutes, or until the crust is golden brown and the cheese is melted and bubbly.

Spicy Sausage Pizza

For the pizza dough:

2 ¼ cups all-purpose flour
1 teaspoon instant yeast
1 teaspoon sugar
1 teaspoon salt
1 cup warm water
2 tablespoons olive oil

For the pizza toppings:

½ cup pizza sauce
2 cups shredded mozzarella cheese
½ pound spicy Italian sausage, cooked and crumbled
¼ cup sliced jalapenos
¼ cup sliced red onion
¼ cup sliced black olives
Crushed red pepper flakes (optional)
Fresh basil leaves, for garnish (optional)

Instructions:

In a large mixing bowl, combine the flour, instant yeast, sugar, and salt. Mix well.
Add the warm water and olive oil to the bowl. Stir until the ingredients are well combined and form a dough.
Transfer the dough onto a floured surface and knead for about 5 minutes until it becomes smooth and elastic. If the dough is too sticky, you can add a little more flour.
Place the dough in a greased bowl and cover it with a damp cloth. Allow it to rise in a warm place for about 1 to 1.5 hours or until it doubles in size.
Preheat your oven to 475°F (245°C) and place a pizza stone or baking sheet in the oven to heat up.
Roll out the risen dough into a round shape to your desired thickness. Carefully transfer it onto a sheet of parchment paper or a pizza peel dusted with flour or cornmeal.
Spread the pizza sauce evenly over the dough, leaving a small border around the edges for the crust.
Sprinkle the shredded mozzarella cheese over the sauce, covering the entire surface.
Distribute the cooked and crumbled spicy Italian sausage, sliced jalapenos, sliced red onion, and sliced black olives evenly over the cheese.
If desired, sprinkle crushed red pepper flakes over the toppings for an extra kick.
Carefully transfer the pizza (with the parchment paper or pizza peel) onto the preheated baking sheet or pizza stone in the oven.
Bake for about 12-15 minutes, or until the crust is golden brown and the cheese is bubbly and slightly browned.
Remove the pizza from the oven and let it cool for a few minutes. Garnish with fresh basil leaves if desired.
Slice and serve the Spicy Sausage Pizza while it's still warm.
Enjoy your delicious and fiery Spicy Sausage Pizza!

Thai Sweet Chili Pork Pizza

For the Thai sweet chili pork:

1 pound ground pork
2 tablespoons Thai sweet chili sauce
2 tablespoons soy sauce
1 tablespoon rice vinegar
1 tablespoon brown sugar
2 cloves garlic, minced
1 teaspoon grated ginger
1 teaspoon sesame oil

For the pizza toppings:

½ cup Thai sweet chili sauce
2 cups shredded mozzarella cheese
½ cup sliced red bell pepper
½ cup sliced red onion
¼ cup chopped fresh cilantro
Crushed red pepper flakes (optional)

Instructions:

In a large mixing bowl, combine the flour, instant yeast, sugar, and salt. Mix well.
Add the warm water and olive oil to the bowl. Stir until the ingredients are well combined and form a dough.
Transfer the dough onto a floured surface and knead for about 5 minutes until it becomes smooth and elastic. If the dough is too sticky, you can add a little more flour.
Place the dough in a greased bowl and cover it with a damp cloth. Allow it to rise in a warm place for about 1 to 1.5 hours or until it doubles in size.
Preheat your oven to 475°F (245°C) and place a pizza stone or baking sheet in the oven to heat up.
In a skillet, heat the sesame oil over medium heat. Add the ground pork and cook until browned and cooked through.
In a small bowl, whisk together the Thai sweet chili sauce, soy sauce, rice vinegar, brown sugar, minced garlic, and grated ginger. Pour the sauce mixture over the cooked ground pork. Stir to coat the pork evenly in the sauce. Cook for an additional 2-3 minutes, allowing the flavors to meld together. Remove from heat and set aside.
Roll out the risen dough into a round shape to your desired thickness. Carefully transfer it onto a sheet of parchment paper or a pizza peel dusted with flour or cornmeal.
Spread the Thai sweet chili sauce evenly over the dough, leaving a small border around the edges for the crust.
Sprinkle the shredded mozzarella cheese over the sauce, covering the entire surface.
Distribute the cooked Thai sweet chili pork, sliced red bell pepper, and sliced red onion evenly over the cheese.
If desired, sprinkle crushed red pepper flakes over the toppings for an extra kick.
Carefully transfer the pizza (with the parchment paper or pizza peel) onto the preheated baking sheet or pizza stone in the oven.
Bake for about 12-15 minutes, or until the crust is golden brown and the cheese is bubbly and slightly browned.
Remove the pizza from the oven and let it cool for a few minutes. Sprinkle chopped fresh cilantro over the pizza.
Slice and serve the Thai Sweet Chili Pork Pizza while it's still warm.
Enjoy your unique and flavorful Thai Sweet Chili Pork Pizza!

Caprese Pizza

Ingredients:

For the pizza dough:
2 ¼ cups all-purpose flour
1 teaspoon instant yeast
1 teaspoon sugar
1 teaspoon salt
1 cup warm water
2 tablespoons olive oil

For the pizza toppings:
½ cup pizza sauce or marinara sauce
2 cups shredded mozzarella cheese
2-3 ripe tomatoes, sliced
8-10 fresh basil leaves
4-5 ounces fresh mozzarella cheese, sliced
Balsamic glaze (optional)
Salt and pepper to taste

Instructions:

In a large mixing bowl, combine the flour, instant yeast, sugar, and salt. Mix well.
Add the warm water and olive oil to the bowl. Stir until the ingredients are well combined and form a dough.
Transfer the dough onto a floured surface and knead for about 5 minutes until it becomes smooth and elastic. If the dough is too sticky, you can add a little more flour.
Place the dough in a greased bowl and cover it with a damp cloth. Allow it to rise in a warm place for about 1 to 1.5 hours or until it doubles in size.
Preheat your oven to 475°F (245°C) and place a pizza stone or baking sheet in the oven to heat up.
Roll out the risen dough into a round shape to your desired thickness. Carefully transfer it onto a sheet of parchment paper or a pizza peel dusted with flour or cornmeal.
Spread the pizza sauce evenly over the dough, leaving a small border around the edges for the crust.
Sprinkle the shredded mozzarella cheese over the sauce, covering the entire surface.
Arrange the sliced tomatoes and fresh basil leaves on top of the cheese.
Place the sliced fresh mozzarella cheese on top of the other toppings.
Season with salt and pepper to taste.
Carefully transfer the pizza (with the parchment paper or pizza peel) onto the preheated baking sheet or pizza stone in the oven.
Bake for about 12-15 minutes, or until the crust is golden brown and the cheese is bubbly and slightly browned.
Remove the pizza from the oven and let it cool for a few minutes. Drizzle balsamic glaze over the pizza, if desired.
Slice and serve the Caprese Pizza while it's still warm.
Enjoy your delicious and fresh Caprese Pizza, with its classic combination of tomatoes, mozzarella, and basil!

Alice Springs Chicken French Bread Pizza

Ingredients:

1 loaf French bread
4 tablespoons butter, softened
1 teaspoon garlic powder
1 cup cooked chicken breast, diced
4 slices bacon, cooked and crumbled
1 cup shredded Monterey Jack cheese
1 cup shredded cheddar cheese
2 green onions, thinly sliced
2 tablespoons honey mustard sauce

Instructions:

Preheat your oven to 375°F (190°C).
Cut the French bread loaf in half lengthwise and place the halves on a baking sheet, cut side up.
In a small bowl, mix together the softened butter and garlic powder. Spread the garlic butter evenly over the cut sides of the French bread.
Sprinkle the diced chicken breast and crumbled bacon evenly over the bread halves.
In a separate bowl, mix together the shredded Monterey Jack and cheddar cheeses. Sprinkle the cheese mixture over the chicken and bacon.
Top with sliced green onions.
Drizzle the honey mustard sauce over the toppings.
Place the baking sheet with the assembled pizza in the preheated oven and bake for about 15-20 minutes, or until the cheese is melted and bubbly, and the bread is crispy on the edges.
Remove from the oven and let it cool for a few minutes.
Slice the Alice Springs Chicken French Bread Pizza into individual servings.
Serve warm and enjoy!
This recipe is a delightful twist on classic French bread pizza, inspired by the Alice Springs Chicken from Outback Steakhouse. It's packed with flavors from chicken, bacon, cheese, and honey mustard sauce.

Hawaiian Pizza

Ingredients:

1 pizza dough (store-bought or homemade)
½ cup pizza sauce or marinara sauce
2 cups shredded mozzarella cheese
8-10 slices of ham, chopped or torn into pieces
1 cup pineapple chunks (fresh or canned), drained
½ cup sliced red onion
¼ cup sliced black olives (optional)
Fresh basil leaves, for garnish (optional)

Instructions:
Preheat your oven to the temperature specified on your pizza dough package or to 475°F (245°C) if using homemade dough.
Roll out the pizza dough to your desired thickness on a floured surface.
Transfer the rolled-out dough onto a pizza stone or baking sheet lined with parchment paper.
Spread the pizza sauce evenly over the dough, leaving a small border around the edges for the crust.
Sprinkle the shredded mozzarella cheese over the sauce, covering the entire surface.
Distribute the chopped or torn ham, pineapple chunks, sliced red onion, and black olives (if using) evenly over the cheese.
Place the pizza in the preheated oven and bake according to the package instructions or for about 12-15 minutes if using homemade dough. The crust should be golden brown and the cheese melted and bubbly.
Remove the pizza from the oven and let it cool for a few minutes.
Garnish with fresh basil leaves, if desired.
Slice and serve the Hawaiian Pizza while it's still warm.
Enjoy the sweet and savory combination of ham and pineapple in this classic Hawaiian Pizza!

Sweet Chili Garlic Chicken Pizza

For the sweet chili garlic chicken

1 pound boneless, skinless chicken breasts, cut into small pieces
3 tablespoons sweet chili sauce
2 tablespoons soy sauce
2 tablespoons honey
2 cloves garlic, minced
1 tablespoon vegetable oil

Ingredients:

For the pizza dough:
2 ¼ cups all-purpose flour
1 teaspoon instant yeast
1 teaspoon sugar
1 teaspoon salt
1 cup warm water
2 tablespoons olive oil

For the pizza toppings:

½ cup pizza sauce or marinara sauce
2 cups shredded mozzarella cheese
½ cup thinly sliced red onion
½ cup thinly sliced bell peppers (any color)
¼ cup chopped fresh cilantro
Crushed red pepper flakes (optional)

Instructions:

In a large mixing bowl, combine the flour, instant yeast, sugar, and salt. Mix well.
Add the warm water and olive oil to the bowl. Stir until the ingredients are well combined and form a dough.
Transfer the dough onto a floured surface and knead for about 5 minutes until it becomes smooth and elastic. If the dough is too sticky, you can add a little more flour.
Place the dough in a greased bowl and cover it with a damp cloth. Allow it to rise in a warm place for about 1 to 1.5 hours or until it doubles in size.
Preheat your oven to 475°F (245°C) and place a pizza stone or baking sheet in the oven to heat up.
In a small bowl, whisk together the sweet chili sauce, soy sauce, honey, and minced garlic to make the sweet chili garlic sauce.
Heat the vegetable oil in a skillet over medium heat. Add the chicken pieces to the skillet and cook until browned and cooked through.
Pour the sweet chili garlic sauce over the cooked chicken in the skillet. Stir to coat the chicken evenly in the sauce.
Cook for an additional 2-3 minutes, allowing the flavors to meld together. Remove from heat and set aside.
Roll out the risen dough into a round shape to your desired thickness. Carefully transfer it onto a sheet of parchment paper or a pizza peel dusted with flour or cornmeal.
Spread the pizza sauce evenly over the dough, leaving a small border around the edges for the crust.
Sprinkle the shredded mozzarella cheese over the sauce, covering the entire surface.
Distribute the cooked sweet chili garlic chicken, thinly sliced red onion, and bell peppers evenly over the cheese.
If desired, sprinkle crushed red pepper flakes over the toppings for an extra kick.
Carefully transfer the pizza (with the parchment paper or pizza peel) onto the preheated baking sheet or pizza stone in the oven.
Bake for about 12-15 minutes, or until the crust is golden brown and the cheese is bubbly and slightly browned.

Philly Cheese Steak Pizza

Ingredients:

For the pizza dough:
2 ¼ cups all-purpose flour
1 teaspoon instant yeast
1 teaspoon sugar
1 teaspoon salt
1 cup warm water
2 tablespoons olive oil

For the Philly cheese steak topping:

1 pound beef sirloin steak, thinly sliced
1 green bell pepper, thinly sliced
1 red bell pepper, thinly sliced
1 onion, thinly sliced
2 cloves garlic, minced
2 tablespoons olive oil
Salt and pepper to taste
1 cup shredded provolone cheese
1 cup shredded mozzarella cheese

For the pizza sauce:

½ cup pizza sauce or marinara sauce

Instructions:

In a large mixing bowl, combine the flour, instant yeast, sugar, and salt. Mix well.
Add the warm water and olive oil to the bowl. Stir until the ingredients are well combined and form a dough.
Transfer the dough onto a floured surface and knead for about 5 minutes until it becomes smooth and elastic. If the dough is too sticky, you can add a little more flour.
Place the dough in a greased bowl and cover it with a damp cloth. Allow it to rise in a warm place for about 1 to 1.5 hours or until it doubles in size.
Preheat your oven to 475°F (245°C) and place a pizza stone or baking sheet in the oven to heat up.
In a skillet, heat 1 tablespoon of olive oil over medium heat. Add the thinly sliced beef steak and cook until browned. Remove the cooked steak from the skillet and set aside.
In the same skillet, add another tablespoon of olive oil. Add the thinly sliced bell peppers, onion, and minced garlic. Sauté until the vegetables are softened. Season with salt and pepper to taste. Remove the cooked vegetables from the skillet and set aside.
Roll out the risen dough into a round shape to your desired thickness. Carefully transfer it onto a sheet of parchment paper or a pizza peel dusted with flour or cornmeal.
Spread the pizza sauce evenly over the dough, leaving a small border around the edges for the crust.
Sprinkle the shredded provolone and mozzarella cheeses over the sauce, covering the entire surface.
Distribute the cooked steak and sautéed vegetables evenly over the cheese.
Carefully transfer the pizza (with the parchment paper or pizza peel) onto the preheated baking sheet or pizza stone in the oven.
Bake for about 12-15 minutes, or until the crust is golden brown and the cheese is bubbly and slightly browned.

Artichoke, Sun Dried Tomatoes and Goat Cheese Pizza

Ingredients:

1 pizza dough (store-bought or homemade)
½ cup pizza sauce or marinara sauce
1 cup shredded mozzarella cheese
1 cup marinated artichoke hearts, drained and chopped
½ cup sun-dried tomatoes, thinly sliced
4 ounces goat cheese, crumbled
Fresh basil leaves, for garnish (optional)
Crushed red pepper flakes, for garnish (optional)

Instructions:
Preheat your oven to the temperature specified on your pizza dough package or to 475°F (245°C) if using homemade dough.
Roll out the pizza dough to your desired thickness on a floured surface.
Transfer the rolled-out dough onto a pizza stone or baking sheet lined with parchment paper.
Spread the pizza sauce evenly over the dough, leaving a small border around the edges for the crust.
Sprinkle the shredded mozzarella cheese over the sauce, covering the entire surface.
Distribute the chopped artichoke hearts and sun-dried tomatoes evenly over the cheese.
Crumble the goat cheese over the toppings, distributing it evenly.
Place the pizza in the preheated oven and bake according to the package instructions or for about 12-15 minutes if using homemade dough. The crust should be golden brown and the cheese melted and bubbly.
Remove the pizza from the oven and let it cool for a few minutes.
Garnish with fresh basil leaves and crushed red pepper flakes, if desired.
Slice and serve the Artichoke, Sun-Dried Tomatoes, and Goat Cheese Pizza while it's still warm.
Enjoy the flavorful combination of artichokes, sun-dried tomatoes, and tangy goat cheese on this delicious pizza!

Prosciutto And Fig Goat Cheese Pizza

Ingredients:

1 pizza dough (store-bought or homemade)
2 tablespoons olive oil
4 ounces goat cheese, crumbled
4-6 slices of prosciutto
4-6 fresh figs, sliced
1 cup arugula
Balsamic glaze, for drizzling (optional)
Salt and pepper, to taste

Instructions:

Preheat your oven to the temperature specified on your pizza dough package or to 475°F (245°C) if using homemade dough.

Roll out the pizza dough to your desired thickness on a floured surface.
Transfer the rolled-out dough onto a pizza stone or baking sheet lined with parchment paper.
Brush the olive oil evenly over the dough, leaving a small border around the edges for the crust.
Sprinkle the crumbled goat cheese over the oiled dough, covering the entire surface.
Tear or slice the prosciutto into smaller pieces and distribute them evenly over the goat cheese.
Arrange the sliced fresh figs on top of the prosciutto.
Season with salt and pepper to taste.
Place the pizza in the preheated oven and bake according to the package instructions or for about 12-15 minutes if using homemade dough. The crust should be golden brown and the cheese melted and bubbly.
Remove the pizza from the oven and let it cool for a few minutes.
Scatter the arugula over the pizza.
Drizzle balsamic glaze over the toppings, if desired.
Slice and serve the Prosciutto and Fig Goat Cheese Pizza while it's still warm.
Enjoy the delightful combination of savory prosciutto, sweet figs, tangy goat cheese, and peppery arugula on this delicious pizza!

Easy Steak Gorgonzola Flatbread Pizza

Ingredients:

2 flatbreads or naan bread
8 ounces cooked steak, thinly sliced
½ cup crumbled Gorgonzola cheese
½ cup shredded mozzarella cheese
¼ cup chopped red onion
¼ cup chopped fresh parsley
Salt and pepper, to taste
Olive oil, for brushing

Instructions:

Preheat your oven to 425°F (220°C).
Place the flatbreads or naan bread on a baking sheet lined with parchment paper.
Brush the flatbreads with a thin layer of olive oil.
Sprinkle the shredded mozzarella cheese evenly over the flatbreads.
Arrange the thinly sliced cooked steak on top of the cheese.
Sprinkle the crumbled Gorgonzola cheese, chopped red onion, and fresh parsley over the steak.
Season with salt and pepper to taste.
Place the baking sheet with the flatbreads in the preheated oven and bake for about 12-15 minutes, or until the cheese is melted and bubbly and the edges of the flatbread are golden brown.
Remove from the oven and let it cool for a few minutes.
Slice the Steak Gorgonzola Flatbread Pizza into smaller pieces.
Serve warm and enjoy!

Caramelized Onion Feta Spinach Pizza with White Sauce

Ingredients:

For the white sauce:
2 tablespoons butter
2 tablespoons all-purpose flour
1 cup milk
Salt and pepper to taste
½ teaspoon dried oregano

For the pizza:

1 pizza dough (store-bought or homemade)
1 cup caramelized onions (see note below)
1 cup baby spinach leaves
½ cup crumbled feta cheese
Olive oil, for drizzling

Instructions:

For the white sauce:
In a small saucepan, melt the butter over medium heat.
Add the flour to the melted butter and whisk continuously for about 1 minute to form a roux.
Gradually pour in the milk while whisking constantly to avoid lumps.
Continue cooking the sauce, stirring frequently, until it thickens to a creamy consistency.
Season with salt, pepper, and dried oregano. Remove from heat and set aside.

For the pizza:
Preheat your oven to the temperature specified on your pizza dough package or to 475°F (245°C) if using homemade dough.
Roll out the pizza dough to your desired thickness on a floured surface.
Transfer the rolled-out dough onto a pizza stone or baking sheet lined with parchment paper.
Spread the white sauce evenly over the dough, leaving a small border around the edges for the crust.
Distribute the caramelized onions evenly over the sauce.
Layer the baby spinach leaves over the onions.
Sprinkle the crumbled feta cheese over the spinach.
Drizzle a little olive oil over the toppings for added flavor.
Place the pizza in the preheated oven and bake according to the package instructions or for about 12-15 minutes if using homemade dough. The crust should be golden brown and the cheese melted and slightly browned.
Remove the pizza from the oven and let it cool for a few minutes.

Ultimate Veggie Pizza

Ingredients:

For the pizza dough:
2 ¼ cups all-purpose flour
1 teaspoon instant yeast
1 teaspoon sugar
1 teaspoon salt
1 cup warm water
2 tablespoons olive oil

For the toppings:

1 cup shredded mozzarella cheese
½ cup sliced bell peppers (red, green, and/or yellow)
½ cup sliced red onion
½ cup sliced mushrooms
½ cup sliced black olives
½ cup sliced cherry tomatoes
½ cup chopped broccoli florets
½ cup baby spinach leaves
2 tablespoons olive oil
Salt and pepper to taste
Grated Parmesan cheese, for sprinkling (optional)

For the pizza sauce:

½ cup pizza sauce or marinara sauce

Instructions:

In a large mixing bowl, combine the flour, instant yeast, sugar, and salt. Mix well.
Add the warm water and olive oil to the bowl. Stir until the ingredients are well combined and form a dough.
Transfer the dough onto a floured surface and knead for about 5 minutes until it becomes smooth and elastic. If the dough is too sticky, you can add a little more flour.
Place the dough in a greased bowl and cover it with a damp cloth. Allow it to rise in a warm place for about 1 to 1.5 hours or until it doubles in size.
Preheat your oven to the temperature specified on your pizza dough package or to 475°F (245°C) if using homemade dough.
Roll out the risen dough into a round shape to your desired thickness. Carefully transfer it onto a sheet of parchment paper or a pizza peel dusted with flour or cornmeal.
Spread the pizza sauce evenly over the dough, leaving a small border around the edges for the crust.
Sprinkle the shredded mozzarella cheese over the sauce, covering the entire surface.
Distribute the sliced bell peppers, red onion, mushrooms, black olives, cherry tomatoes, chopped broccoli florets, and baby spinach leaves evenly over the cheese.
Drizzle the olive oil over the toppings and season with salt and pepper to taste.
Place the pizza (with the parchment paper or pizza peel) onto a baking sheet or pizza stone in the preheated oven.
Bake for about 12-15 minutes or until the crust is golden brown and the cheese is melted and bubbly.
Remove the pizza from the oven and let it cool for a few minutes.
Sprinkle with grated Parmesan cheese, if desired.
Slice and serve the Ultimate Veggie Pizza while it's still warm.
Enjoy the abundance of fresh vegetables and cheesy goodness in this delicious Ultimate Veggie Pizza!

Easy Mediterranean Pizza

Ingredients:
For the pizza dough:

2 ¼ cups all-purpose flour
1 teaspoon instant yeast
1 teaspoon sugar
1 teaspoon salt
1 cup warm water
2 tablespoons olive oil

For the toppings:

½ cup pizza sauce or marinara sauce
1 ½ cups shredded mozzarella cheese
½ cup sliced cherry tomatoes
½ cup sliced Kalamata olives
½ cup crumbled feta cheese
¼ cup chopped red onion
¼ cup chopped fresh basil leaves
2 tablespoons extra virgin olive oil
Salt and pepper to taste
Crushed red pepper flakes (optional)

Instructions:

In a large mixing bowl, combine the flour, instant yeast, sugar, and salt. Mix well.
Add the warm water and olive oil to the bowl. Stir until the ingredients are well combined and form a dough.
Transfer the dough onto a floured surface and knead for about 5 minutes until it becomes smooth and elastic. If the dough is too sticky, you can add a little more flour.
Place the dough in a greased bowl and cover it with a damp cloth. Allow it to rise in a warm place for about 1 to 1.5 hours or until it doubles in size.
Preheat your oven to the temperature specified on your pizza dough package or to 475°F (245°C) if using homemade dough.
Roll out the risen dough into a round shape to your desired thickness. Carefully transfer it onto a sheet of parchment paper or a pizza peel dusted with flour or cornmeal.
Spread the pizza sauce evenly over the dough, leaving a small border around the edges for the crust.
Sprinkle the shredded mozzarella cheese over the sauce, covering the entire surface.
Distribute the sliced cherry tomatoes, Kalamata olives, crumbled feta cheese, chopped red onion, and chopped basil leaves evenly over the cheese.
Drizzle the extra virgin olive oil over the toppings. Season with salt and pepper to taste.
Place the pizza (with the parchment paper or pizza peel) onto a baking sheet or pizza stone in the preheated oven.
Bake for about 12-15 minutes, or until the crust is golden brown and the cheese is melted and bubbly.
Remove the pizza from the oven and let it cool for a few minutes.
Sprinkle with crushed red pepper flakes for an extra kick, if desired.
Slice and serve the Easy Mediterranean Pizza while it's still warm.
Enjoy the Mediterranean flavors of tomatoes, olives, feta cheese, and fresh basil on this delicious pizza!

Shrimp Scampi Pizza

Ingredients:

For the pizza dough:
2 ¼ cups all-purpose flour
1 teaspoon instant yeast
1 teaspoon sugar
1 teaspoon salt
1 cup warm water
2 tablespoons olive oil

For the shrimp scampi topping:

1 pound large shrimp, peeled and deveined
4 cloves garlic, minced
2 tablespoons butter
2 tablespoons olive oil
2 tablespoons lemon juice
Zest of 1 lemon
Salt and pepper to taste
½ cup shredded mozzarella cheese
¼ cup grated Parmesan cheese
¼ cup chopped fresh parsley

Instructions:

For the pizza dough:
In a large mixing bowl, combine the flour, instant yeast, sugar, and salt. Mix well.
Add the warm water and olive oil to the bowl. Stir until the ingredients are well combined and form a dough.
Transfer the dough onto a floured surface and knead for about 5 minutes until it becomes smooth and elastic. If the dough is too sticky, you can add a little more flour.
Place the dough in a greased bowl and cover it with a damp cloth. Allow it to rise in a warm place for about 1 to 1.5 hours or until it doubles in size.

For the shrimp scampi topping:
Preheat your oven to the temperature specified on your pizza dough package or to 475°F (245°C) if using homemade dough.
In a skillet, melt the butter and olive oil over medium heat. Add the minced garlic and sauté for about 1 minute until fragrant.
Add the shrimp to the skillet and cook for 2-3 minutes on each side until they turn pink and opaque. Remove from heat.
Stir in the lemon juice, lemon zest, salt, and pepper. Set aside.

Assembling the pizza:
Roll out the risen pizza dough into a round shape to your desired thickness. Carefully transfer it onto a sheet of parchment paper or a pizza peel dusted with flour or cornmeal.
Spread the shrimp scampi mixture evenly over the dough, leaving a small border around the edges for the crust.
Sprinkle the shredded mozzarella cheese and grated Parmesan cheese over the shrimp.
Place the pizza (with the parchment paper or pizza peel) onto a baking sheet or pizza stone in the preheated oven.
Bake for about 12-15 minutes, or until the crust is golden brown and the cheese is melted and bubbly.
Remove the pizza from the oven and let it cool for a few minutes.
Sprinkle with chopped fresh parsley.

Bonus

How To Make The Best Pizza Dough

If you love delicious pizza, then learning how to make your own dough is essential. Here's a quick guide to get you started on your delicious pizza-making journey.

To begin, gather the ingredients needed for pizza dough: all-purpose flour, yeast, warm water, salt and olive oil. Measure out one and a half cups of flour into a large mixing bowl and add two teaspoons of active dry yeast. Pour in three-quarters cup of warm water and whisk until smooth. Stir in one teaspoon of salt and two tablespoons of olive oil before kneading the dough with your hands until it forms a ball. Alternatively, use an electric mixer with a dough hook attachment or food processor to mix the ingredients together.

Once the dough is mixed and kneaded, cover the bowl with plastic wrap and let it rise for about an hour. After that, your delicious pizza dough is ready to use for all sorts of delicious pizza recipes! To shape your pizzas, lightly flour a surface and roll out the dough until you reach the desired size and shape. Top with delicious toppings of your choice, then bake in a preheated oven at 425°F for 15-20 minutes or until golden brown. Enjoy your delicious homemade pizza!

Now that you have mastered how to make delicious pizza dough, you can get creative with different recipes and toppings - giving you endless possibilities when it comes to delicious homemade pizzas. Get started today on your delicious pizza-making journey!

Guidelines:

1. Always make sure to use the correct measurements of ingredients when making pizza dough. This will ensure your delicious homemade pizzas turn out perfect every time.
2. When rolling out your dough, lightly flour a surface and roll until you reach the desired size and shape.
3. Preheat oven to 425°F before baking, then bake for 15-20 minutes or until golden brown.
4. Allow the dough to rise for about an hour before forming into a ball for baking - this allows for delicious flavor development in your pizza crusts!
5. Get creative with different delicious recipes and toppings - giving you endless possibilities when it comes to delicious homemade pizzas.
6. Enjoy your delicious homemade pizza!

Follow these simple steps and you will be making delicious, homemade pizzas in no time! With a little practice, you'll be an expert pizza maker - enjoying delicious recipes with friends and family in no time. Bon appétit!

I want to take a moment to express my heartfelt gratitude for your recent purchase of my recipe book. As a passionate food lover, nothing makes me happier than sharing my favorite recipes with others. Your decision to invest in my book not only supports my dream, but also shows your commitment to expanding your culinary horizons.

I sincerely hope that the recipes in the book will inspire you to try new things and add some excitement to your meals.

Thank you again for your support and for being a part of this journey with me. I hope my book will bring you many happy and delicious moments in the kitchen.

www.ingramcontent.com/pod-product-compliance
Lightning Source LLC
Chambersburg PA
CBHW081126080526
44587CB00021B/3764